CH00967774

Guide to Becoming a Freelance Writer

Use Freelancing Websites to Source Content Writing Jobs and Make Money from Home!

Rhea Gaur

Table of Contents

2

CHAPTER 1: ARE YOU READY TO BE A FREELANCE CONTENT WRITER?

1.1 What Does a Content Writer Do?

Today all businesses need to have an online presence – website, blogs and social media accounts. But most business owners have neither the skill nor the time to create content, which means that there is a big demand for generation of online content. That's where you the content writer can be of service.

Having understood your client's business (product or service, target customer, competitors and content need), as a freelance writer, you will be responsible for creating the following types of content:

- **Website content** – Content you read on various pages of a website.
- **Blogs** – Posts on informative and current topics about the client's business, which would be compelling to its customers.
- **Marketing Emails** – Emails that companies design to promote their products and services. It could be a monthly e-newsletter or an ad-hoc promotional email.
- **Social media updates** – Short posts and images for Facebook, Instagram, Pinterest accounts of the business.

- **eBooks** – An eBook that the client wants to either sell or offer free on their website.
- **Press release** - Online press releases for new products or major changes in the company.

There are other writing opportunities within the **freelance business writing space** as well. These include –

- News summaries
- Brochures
- Promotional flyer
- Process manuals
- Training material
- Academic papers
- Reports
- Business proposals
- Product descriptions
- Company profiles
- Case studies
- Online quizzes

Please note that most of these writing assignments involve 'ghost writing,' which means that you won't get credit for writing the content.

To begin with, you need three essential skills to become a freelance content writer -

- An excellent command of written English.
- Ability to research topics on the web, and
- Ability to present information in a logical, easy-to-read manner

As you start working, you will need to develop the following skills to be successful at freelance content writing.

- **UK and US English:** Understand the differences between the UK and US English.
- **Grammar and Punctuation:** Use the right grammar and punctuation to save your clients the expense of hiring someone to proof-read your work.
- **Research:** You must have the ability to research the topic online, pick the most relevant bits, and present information in a concise/ logical manner.
- **Copywriting skills:** As a freelance writer, you will write for businesses from different industries. One day you are writing for an event-planning website, and the next day you are blogging for a company that sells software. Your writing must engage your client's target

audience. Also, your writing style will vary with what you are writing.

- **Professionalism:** You need to be a thorough professional - ask the right questions to understand what the client wants, deliver high-quality content, meet agreed deadlines, and be prompt in reverting to customer messages/ calls.

- **Multi-tasking:** You need to be adept at managing the various facets of your writing business. You will be responsible for marketing yourself, bidding for projects, delivering the content and following up with clients for payments. Customer service will be a daily part of your job profile as a freelance writer.

- **Positive attitude:** Freelance writing is a competitive business. You are competing with writers from across the world – writers who are more experienced; who are 'native' English speakers; and writers from Asian/African countries who are willing to do the job for a lesser price. It can be difficult to get the first break and to find clients that offer regular paying work. A 'never say die' attitude will keep you going through the tough initial months.

- **Familiarity with online tools:** Clients expect you to be familiar with the latest online writing tools and digital marketing terminology. Spend a few hours every week researching what's new and how you can build your knowledge to add value to your clients.

- **Originality:** Your writing style is what sets you apart from others. You may not realize it, but you already have a writing style. Build on it, rather than trying to ape somebody.

- **Time management**: As the lone wolf driving your business, meeting deadlines can be challenging. You will need to be adept at time management to ensure you are a 100 percent on time for your clients.

1.3 The Risks and Rewards of Freelance Writing

As with any profession, freelance writing has its pros and cons. Before you quit your job to become a freelance writer, you need to understand what it's like to be one.

- **The world is your competition** - When you choose to become a freelancer on the World Wide Web, you take on the challenge of competing on a global stage. You will compete with freelance writers from North America, Asia, Australia, Africa and Europe. The bidding war revolves around each writer's skills, experience, price and proposed delivery date.

- **You need to take care of everything** – With the thrill of being a business owner, comes added responsibility. You are the strategist, salesperson, marketer, social media specialist, customer service, and operations specialist. You have to know it all and do it all!

- **It's a constant struggle to find business** - You will be continually seeking new clients and trying to bring in more work from existing clients. You will be lucky if your sales pitch conversion rate is more than eight to ten percent of customers contacted.

- **Forget weekends** - Saturday and Sunday are no longer sanctimonious as days where you can take off. There will be days of no work, followed by days where there is more work than you can handle. So you work when you have to, which may include weekends.

- **Time is even harder to come by** - Yes there is greater flexibility for fulfilling personal commitments, but time is as scarce as ever. As a freelance writer, you are multitasking for most of your work day and time just flies. You need to cross-check your planner continuously for delivery schedules, making sure you stay on track.

- **You earn as long as you work** - Quitting the comfort of a well-paying job to start your venture is fraught with uncertainties. Forget the comfort of a healthy bank balance at the end of each month, also known as the salary. As a freelance writer, if you aren't working, you aren't earning.

But being a freelance writer has its rewards. It's exciting to get a new contract, work with international clients, write for different businesses, earn in dollars while working from home, and to see your writing help businesses achieve their goals.

As a freelance writer, you no longer have to contend with long commutes to work, attend business meetings that seem never ending, or go through the dreaded annual appraisal. You choose whom you want to work with and how much work you want to take on. You can work from anywhere, anytime. Doing your own thing gives you a satisfaction that no 9 to 5 job can match.

So should you jump on the freelancing bandwagon? Having weighed the pros and cons of life as a freelancer, this is a question that only you can answer. Although you will receive well-meaning advice from family and friends, it has to be ultimately your call. If you can cope with the 'uncertainty' of how much you will earn by when (especially in the initial phase), then freelance writing offers you an exciting opportunity to be the captain of your ship. But, if you aren't motivated enough to stay focused and work all by yourself, then you will find the going rough in the turbulent world of freelance writing.

CHAPTER 2. STARTING AS A FREELANCE CONTENT WRITER

Congratulations on choosing freelance writing as your entrepreneurial venture. You now have a fair understanding of the risks of being a freelancer and want to make a go of it. So, let's create your writing business.

2.1 Understand How to Write for the Web

There are three important things you must know when writing for the web.

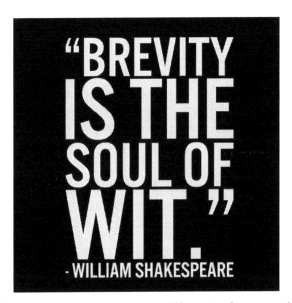

1. **Writing for the web is different from writing content for print.**

   A person who picks up a magazine is willing to spend both money and time to read what you have to say. In most print publications, the articles tend to be lengthy, with verbose paragraphs and sentences.

In contrast, the average web reader spends only a few seconds on any website, before he decides to either continue reading or to move to another website. Because you have little time in which to make an impression, you need to ensure that the online content is easy to read and engaging, without the use of unnecessary/ decorative words and phrases. Most articles written for the web have a succinct article headline, subheadings, bullet points, and highlighted text.

2. **Web content has to be search engine optimized.** Search engine optimization or SEO is the primary goal of all online content written for businesses. SEO techniques improve the likelihood of the company's website appearing on search engines such as Google and Bing when someone searches for related information.

As a web content writer, you must have a basic understanding of SEO techniques in content development.

Here are two tips for developing content that is SEO friendly.

Technique 1 – Focus on quality and frequency of content

Both the quality of content and the frequency of new content updated, are important for a website's SEO rankings. Genuine content updated at a regular frequency is good for the website's SEO ranking.

As the online content writer, it is your job to identify and write on topics that are of interest to potential customers. For example, a website selling air tickets can do a series of posts on the facilities at international and domestic airports. The assumption is that someone looking for information on an airport is also going to need air tickets sometime soon, which is how the website can pitch its service.

Plagiarized content and lack of fresh content lowers a website's SEO ranking.

Technique 2 – Include keywords, meta description, and anchor text

To improve SEO rankings, you need to ensure that the content includes 'keywords,' 'meta description', and links to websites of repute.

- **Long tail keywords** are phrases that people looking for a particular information type on their browser. For instance, if you want information on 'teething problems in infants', that online search phrase becomes a keyword for an article on child health problems. Google AdWords – Keyword Planner is a popular tool to search for popular search keywords.
- **Meta description** is the short article summary that appears along with the article link on the search engine page. It tells the reader what the article is about even before they click on the website link. As a thumb rule, the meta description should be about 150-160 characters (including spaces).
- **Anchor texts** are words which have a clickable hyperlink to either another page on the same website

or to a page on another site. The idea is to give readers more information by linking a section of your content to another relevant page.

3. **Style of writing varies with the type of web content** you are writing. For a blog, the preferred style is to write as though you were having a conversation with someone. When you write website content, the writing needs to have more of a salesmanship approach without trying to make a hard sell. An e-book, such as this one, has to informative and easy to scan through for relevant information.

Learning how to write for the web is an art in itself. So here's what you need to do.

Go to your preferred online shopping website and order this ultimate guide for writing online content. It's called - **The Yahoo! Style Guide: The Ultimate Sourcebook for Writing, Editing, and Creating Content for the Digital World** (Priced around $12). The Yahoo! Style Guide is the best upfront investment to kick-start your freelance writing career, apart from the book you are reading ☺.

Order the book now.

Done?

Great, let's take the next step towards starting your freelance career.

2.2 Build Your Writing Portfolio

You know you can write for the web, but to win your first writing project, you need to prove that to your future clients. For that, you need a writing portfolio.

Writing a complete article can be hard, especially if you have never written before or if you haven't written for a while.

Here are a few tips on writing your first batch of articles -

- **Write topics you know**. Derive inspiration from your professional and personal experiences. For instance, if you have worked as a banker, write tips on saving money. If you are a new mom, write about your recent pregnancy experience. If you know a lot about keeping dogs as pets, write about that.
- **Write from experience, but do your research**. Search online articles and blogs written on your topic. Include recent trends or statistics to make the material more current.
- **Include at least one anchor text link to another website of repute** in your article. Again, this is good SEO practice.

- **Keep the writing style easy**. Use words that you would use when speaking to someone. Don't use jargons.
- **Ask a friend or a family member to read your articles.** Rewrite the article if your test group does not understand what the article is about by just looking at the header or by reading the first few lines.

Have a portfolio of at least five articles of about 500-600 words each, before you start bidding for projects on freelancing websites.

Give your portfolio a professional look. Upload your articles on sites like Contently and email the link to potential clients. Also include the portfolio link in your email sign-off.

Before you read further, jot down ten potential topics you can write on.

Now let's dive into the meaty part of this guide – making your way in the daunting world of freelancing websites.

2.3 Using Freelancing Websites to Start as a Freelance Writer

Freelancing websites such as Upwork (formed by merging Odesk and Elance), Freelancer and Guru have made it easy for freelancers to reach clients all over the world. Businesses and individuals post scores of jobs on these websites every day.

More than 3 million freelancing jobs (including non-writing jobs) are available on Upwork annually. These are the types of content writing jobs available on Upwork under the category of writing.

- Academic Writing & Research
- Article & Blog Writing
- Copywriting
- Creative Writing
- Editing & Proofreading
- Grant Writing
- Resumes & Cover Letters

- Technical Writing
- Web Content
- Other – Writing

To start as a freelance writer, all you need to do is to register as a 'contractor' and begin bidding for jobs on the freelancing websites.

2.3.1 Five Benefits of Using Freelancing Websites

Getting a writing assignment through freelance job website is not easy. For every content writing job posted on a freelancing job site, there are hundreds of writers whose skills are a potential match. There are nearly 600,000 writers registered on Upwork alone. Although not every eligible writer applies for each job, you can expect 15 to 20 applicants per job. In some cases, the number of writers pitching for the job goes up to 50 to 60.

Freelance writers from North America and Europe begrudge the lower rates bid by writers from other parts of the world. But contractors from Asia and Africa often lose out on projects because they are not native English speakers.

Most content writing jobs on the freelancing websites are for ghost-writing, which means that you will not get credit for the words written. And unless you are careful in choosing your clients, you could end up having a nasty experience. The client may not pay or leave negative comments on your online profile.

But regardless of the challenges and drawbacks of using freelance job websites, these sites offer the immense benefits for aspiring freelance writers.

Five Benefits of Using Freelancing Websites

- **Global reach with minimal cost:** Freelancing websites give you access to international clients across myriad businesses, without having to spend a significant amount. Most websites have free membership plans to get you started. Paid membership plans that allow you to bid for a higher number of jobs, start as low as $10 a month.

- **Project management:** These websites allow you to manage all interactions with the client on a single platform. The project management features of freelancing websites include milestone setting, project reports, invoice generation, reminders, and inbox messaging.

- **Secure payment:** Almost all sites have an escrow payment guarantee system. Before the work starts, the client funds the project in full or as per dollar value of each agreed project milestone. Once you submit the content and raise an invoice through the website, the client must release the escrow amount to your account. Important – ensure that the customer funds escrow before you start working on the project.

- **Dispute resolution:** The messaging system records all communications between you and the clients. If there is a dispute, the freelance sites also have a complaints resolution system, which collects feedback from both parties (client and the contractor) and notifies of a decision.

- **Opportunity to understand your competition –** These websites are a great way to get a sneak peek into the skills, writing samples, and pricing of other writers, and to assess your competitiveness as a freelance writer. Just take a look at the profile of other writers bidding for the same projects as you.

2.3.2 What is the Cost of Using Freelancing Websites?

The cost of using freelancing websites has two components –

- **Membership fee:** Popular freelance job websites such as Upwork, Freelancer, and Guru have free membership plans that allow you to bid on a few projects. But given the low rate of successfully bidding for projects, you will need to upgrade to a paid membership plan to be able to apply for more writing jobs.

- **Website Commission:** Most websites deduct a fee of 8 to 10 percent from your project earnings. To circumvent this fee, add the website fee to your article rate. To earn $20 per article, bid at $22 for each article to the client, so you make a net amount of $20 after the $2 deduction of website commission.

You also lose a small amount of your earnings in the form of currency conversion rate, when you withdraw money from the freelancing website to the bank account. That's because the exchange rate to sell dollars (which is what you do when you convert your USD earnings to the local currency) is always lower than the exchange rate to buy dollars.

2.3.3 Eight Tips on Creating a Stellar Profile on Freelancing Websites

The word freelancer has its origins from the 18th century, as 'available for hire mercenaries who possessed fighting weapons or lances'.

The one weapon that you as the modern day freelancer have is your profile on the freelance job website. Your freelance profile is the world's window to you. It should do a good job of selling your skills and telling the client why they should hire you.

Here are eight tips for creating a strong contractor profile on any freelancing website.

1) **Upload a professional picture** – Clients want to know who they are hiring. Your profile photo must be clear and professional looking. As an example, many fitness instructors who are also freelance writers have profile pictures which show their whole body. That's because a client who wants content for a fitness website is more likely to hire a writer who is also a fitness enthusiast.

2) **Develop a concise tagline** – The profile tag line is a synopsis of your expertise. Use less than five words to summarize and sell your skills as a freelance writer. For instance – 'Health, Lifestyle, and Finance Writer.'

3) **Describe your services, skills, and experience** – Describe your services, professional experience and

educational qualifications on your profile page. Include anything that could be a 'value addition' to your profile. If you love to grow vegetables, that could be of interest to a client looking for content on organic farming. As a new mom, you may be just what a nanny agency wants in the writer they hire.

4) **Sell yourself; don't just describe what you do** - Why should the client hire you? What makes you better than other writers? Use your copyrighting skills to sell yourself.

5) **Upload your portfolio** – Upload the sample articles written by you. As you gain experience, add new articles to your portfolio. But do not upload articles that you have ghost written.

6) **Take the skills test** – Depending on the skills you are listing, take the online skill-validation tests available on the freelancing websites. In particular English U.K, English U.S skills tests are crucial for non-native English speakers. The scores of these tests appear on your freelancing website profile as proof of your skill. If you don't do well, don't worry. You can retake the tests.

7) **Ask for feedback** – On completion of each project, ask the client for feedback comments and satisfaction rating to improve your contractor profile on the

freelancing websites. Return the favour by leaving feedback for the client.

8) **Reinvent your profile every few months** – As you complete more writing assignments, you become a better writer and that must show on your profile. Update your profile every three or four months to highlight all new skills acquired.

With your writer profile in place, the time has come to start bidding for projects.

2.3.4 Ten Tips for Successfully Bidding on Freelancing Website

To bid for a project, each writer (known as the 'contractor' on the freelancing website) has to submit his/her proposal to the client. The proposal is only visible to the client.

A proposal describes why the contractor should be awarded the project, how they would handle the job, the proposed cost, and the time it would take to complete the project.

Every bid that you make for a job on the freelancing website must include the following:

- Who you are and why you are the best person for the job?
- Your relevant experience
- Samples of similar content written

25

- How much you will charge, and
- Your approach for handling the project

Here are ten tips for making successful project bids on freelancing websites-

1) **Understand the project requirements** – While submitting your proposal, answer every question/ concern raised by the client in the job post. Some clients may ask you to quote a random word or sentence as part of your proposal to check if you've read the complete job post.

2) **Know the client** – Some customers prefer to work with established contractors (i.e. those with experience and established customer ratings on the freelancing website). Most are open to working with new writers as long as they can prove the skills to do the job. Here are some ways to know your future client -

   - Look for the person's name. The name could be part of the job description posted by the client. It may also be mentioned on the client's profile page on the freelancing website. Address the client by name in the proposal, where possible.
   - Read the client's website or any other link available in the job listing to ensure you understand the business.

- Check the client profile page for how much the client paid for similar jobs in the past.
- Read client reviews from other contractors who have worked with the client and the kind of reviews the client has left for other contractors. Does the client seem like a fair and helpful employer?
- To ensure that the client can pay for your services, check if he has verified a payment method on the website.

3) **Customize your proposal for each job** – You have no more than a few seconds to grab the client's attention and convince them to read your entire proposal. Although it's good to give the necessary information (who you are, your specialization, portfolio, cost), explain why you are the best person for the job. Use highlighted text and bullet points to quickly sell yourself as the best candidate.

4) **Attach relevant writing samples with each proposal** – Attach samples of your past work that are relevant to the job. If you haven't written on that subject before, attach a sample that is closest to the writing style required for the job.

5) **Propose a T + 1 timeframe for completion of the job** – Missing an agreed deadline can result in negative customer feedback on your profile. Always negotiate a timeline with the client that is T+1 (number

of days), with T being your internal deadline and T + 1 being what you agree with the client.

If need be, ask the client for more information on the project so you can set a realistic project timeline. Some clients want the job done within the day. Unless you are a subject matter expert or a hundred percent sure that you can meet the tight deadline, stay away from such jobs.

6) **Be flexible in your pricing** – Pricing is crucial in determining your success in winning projects. Take the following aspects into consideration while proposing pricing –

   - The project budget indicated by the client
   - Is it a client you have worked for before and is the client worth retaining?
   - Is there potential for long-term work with the client?
   - How much time would it take to research and write the content?
   - Is the client willing to publish your name as the writer?

7) **Don't underbid for projects** – Most clients indicate a project budget for the job; don't under-quote the price to win the contract. Understand that the project price has to match the amount of time you are going to spend on it. By under-bidding, not only do you make it

difficult for yourself and every other writer trying to make a decent living, but you may also harm your profile ranking by underbidding on the website.

8) **Negotiate until you are comfortable** – Don't hesitate to negotiate the project timeline, payment method (hourly versus fixed fee) and project milestones (dates and payments). When working with a new client or on a project that will be more than a week, ensure that you create milestones for submission of work and collection of payment.

9) **Don't take unpaid trial assignments** – A genuine client will pay for your work even if it's a single test assignment. Your writing samples are proof of your skill, so under no circumstance should you write for free.

10) **Don't stop bidding for better jobs** – Long-term projects can run dry without warning. Don't stop looking for more work or better-paying work. Continue to market yourself.

Here is a sample proposal:

Hello Paul,

I am a former banking professional, with experience of more than 14 years across global organizations such as ABN AMRO Bank N.V & Standard Chartered Bank. I have been a full-time freelance writer for about five years.

29

Two very good reasons why you should allow me to work for you:

1. Am currently rated in top 2% of service providers in the category of writing which vouches for quality of my work.

2. I have written more than 100 articles in the business technology and online marketing niche and am confident of writing content that will engage your target audience.

Samples *- My understanding is that your requirement is in the business technology niche. Hence enclosing relevant samples.*

1. I have successfully written for Ramon Ray, a technology evangelist helping small businesses do more! Ramon has also been recognized by mashable.com as one of the best Twitter accounts for Entrepreneurs (@ramonray). These are directly posted by me on the WP site. Given below are links to some of the relevant articles.

http://www.smallbiztechnology.com/archive/2013/03/survey-reveals-three-trends-to-follow-to-successful-internet-marketing.html/

http://www.smallbiztechnology.com/archive/2013/09/safeguard-your-business-with-mobility-management-software.html/

2. *Blog written for a UK software company on Google Glass application development. (file attached)*

How I recommend handling the project:

- *Request you to give a download on your business, competitors, target segment, and preferred writing style.*
- *Escrow to be funded prior to start of each agreed project milestone.*
- *Each article will be accompanied by a relevant article heading, subheading and researched article links.*
- *All content will be written by me and run through Copyscape before submitting.*
- *Payment will be requested on successful completion of each agreed milestone.*
- *Release of payment will be considered as final acceptance of content.*

My bid: *$30 (excluding Upwork fee) for each article of 400 words.*

I have worked successfully with clients in the UK, US, Canada and Australia. I hope you will consider employing my services as well.

Best regards,

Once the client expresses interest in hiring you for the project, a process of negotiation, where you agree on final pricing, delivery dates and project milestones (i.e. by when will you deliver how much content).

After the client awards the contract to you, set up the milestones on the freelancing website and seek escrow funding for the first milestone. Begin writing when you see the escrow funded.

Submit your work to the client by uploading files in the project workroom. As you complete each project milestone, send a status sheet to the client through the freelance website. When the client confirms acceptance of the work submitted, raise an invoice through the freelancing website and ask the client to fund the next milestone.

2.3.5 Five Aspects to Consider Before Working with a Client

One of the perks of being a freelance writer is getting to choose your clients. But how do you decide which client is worth pursuing and who isn't?

Most projects involve the following sequential engagement with the client.

Project Proposal > Messaging> Project Awarded > Milestone Setting > Commence Writing

The second stage of messaging is the time for you to decide whether the client and the project are worth pursuing. It is at this juncture that you will be able to review the match between your skills and project.

Here are five things which you need to consider before working with a new client:

1. **Project detailing:** How well has the client described the project requirements? A client who has made the effort to detail the project is someone who knows what they want. Such clients are unlikely to waste your time by asking for major rework.

2. **Client's communication style:** Does the client's message begin with a 'hello' and does he address you by name? Has the client taken the time to explain things and ask the right questions from you? Is he quick in responding to your initial messages? A client who values freelancers as business partners and not as cheap labour will tick all these checks.

3. **Flexibility in approach:** Most clients respect that you are not just waiting for them to give you work. They are willing to extend deadlines if need be. They will also allow a free-hand in the way you want to execute the project as long as you follow some basic guidelines. But if the client is rigid in the way he wants the project handled, then before you take on the project ensure that you are in a position to deliver as per expectations.

4. **Price negotiation:** Is the client willing to pay for a trial article? Clients who offer a paid sample assignment are any day better than clients that want you to quote the 'best rates' (read lowest) at the start of the project. Some clients may try to push down your fee by

promising to give you bulk work in the future. Unfortunately, such promises rarely come to fruition.

5. **Client's reputation:** Assess the client's reputation on the website. View the number of jobs posted and awarded by the client, reviews written by the client for other contractors, the general tone of reviews, and the feedback by contractors on their experience of working with the client.

Consider other aspects as well. Perhaps the client needs the work sooner than you had planned for, or perhaps the work requires more hours of research than initially indicated. Evaluate your level of comfort in writing in the required niche. Is there long-term work potential with the client, and is the client is willing to give you credit (i.e. publish your name as the writer)?

Even though it's always great to have repeat business from clients, ensure that you continue to safeguard your interests on new projects. Always agree on interim milestones with the client and request for escrow funding for each milestone.

2.3.6 Should You Have a Writing Niche?

As a new freelance writer, the best subjects to write on are those where you have some level of expertise, experience, or interest. If you have always been a fitness enthusiast or someone who advises friends on how to stay in shape, then writing on fitness topics will come easy. Not only are you writing from personal experience, but you will also know the information to research.

As you gain experience writing for clients, you realise that you can research and write on any topic under the sun. With time, you also begin to branch out to other topics, styles, and formats of writing.

So why should you develop a writing niche? **A writing niche is important because it becomes your selling point, especially when you are pitching for work with new clients.** Being able to call yourself a subject matter expert, gives you room for asking for a higher article fee.

But writing outside your niche, makes you a better writer. Writing on broader topics also gives you a chance to widen your client base.

If you can manage it, do both. Have a niche that becomes your talking point, and try to write for as wide array for clients as possible. Pick a that strategy works best for you.

2.3.7 Five Tips on How Much to Charge as a Freelance Writer

When you start as a freelance writer, one of the first questions on your mind is, "How much should I charge for my writing services?".

Finding an answer to this issue can be difficult. Unlike other jobs or corporate designations, there is no known pay structure that you can reference. Also, it's difficult to benchmark yourself against other writers. Every writer has unique skills, both in the type of content they write and their quality of writing. Someone who is just starting out can expect to earn much lesser than an established niche writer.

Content writing job rates vary from $10 to $50 per 500 words depending on the type of content and the size of the business you are writing for.

How much you should charge for a project will depend on things such as the quantum of work the client is offering, the amount of research you will need to do, and the client's business. For instance, writing rates for content on personal development (e.g. self-improvement, overcoming adversity) and lifestyle topics (e.g. fitness, green living) are lower than writing rates for business topics like banking services, software design, and business analytics.

Here are five tips for how much you should charge for your freelance writing services. -

1) **Decide your most reasonable price:** Clients are willing to pay more for your work once you have either worked with them or when they see high customer ratings from other clients. Since you have neither of these when you start writing, quote your minimum price when you start bidding for projects. Remember the aim is to get the job and gradually build a client base.

2) **Review freelancing websites for how much others are charging:** To get an idea of competition, look at the minimum hourly rates of other writers with similar experience as yours. Another way is to compare the price you have bid with the price range of other bids received for the project.

3) **Charge higher if you have relevant experience:** As a writer you have an edge if the current project you are bidding for is a niche that you have written on. You may want to bid higher than your usual price on such projects. But don't be so unrealistic in your demands that your writing rate becomes uncompetitive.

4) **Consider the client relationship:** Different clients will pay different amounts for the same type of work. For instance, clients in India tend to have lower budgets than clients in the US or the UK. When an existing client has a lower budget, consider other aspects of the work-relationship, such as the ease of working with the client, their promptness in clearing invoices, and the potential for future work. Some flexibility in pricing is good.

5) **Increase your fee gradually:** As you work with clients across industries and build a reputation as a writer, you want to charge more. But how often should you increase your rates? With existing clients, once a year, or once every two years, is a good enough time before asking for an increase. Some clients will agree readily to the revised fee while others will negotiate with you further. There is always the risk that some clients will refuse to accept the revised rate and take their business elsewhere.

Speak to your clients or send them an email at least two months in advance of the date from when you want to hike your rates. Also communicate your willingness to work at the new fee for the next 'X' months.

Word of warning - Some clients may offer projects at a low fee in exchange for five-star ratings to boost your profile. You need to decide if you want to work for pittance. Your time is worth something, and it is up to you to set your minimum writing fee.

2.3.8 How to Withdraw Earnings from the Freelancing Website to Your Bank

You have just finished your first writing assignment, and now it's time to enjoy the fruits of your labour a.k.a – the money!

Here's what you need to do –

- Raise an invoice through the freelancing website for the work completed
- Basis the invoice, the client will release the funds from the escrow account
- This amount will now reflect as your account balance on the website. Withdraw the money via a bank transfer or PayPal

PayPal is a safe and quick way of withdrawing your money. Once the freelance website transfers the money to your PayPal account in US Dollars (USD), PayPal transfers the money to your bank account in the local currency, which takes less than five business days.

Withdrawing funds via PayPal may cost you depending on the freelance website of your choice. For instance, Upwork charges $1.00 per transaction to send your earnings to PayPal. Freelancer has free withdrawals to PayPal.

PayPal does not charge anything for transferring money from your PayPal account to your bank account. But, it uses a 'USD to local currency' conversion rate that is lower than the market rate (that's how they make money from the transaction).

PayPal is still faster and cheaper than routing the funds to your bank through a wire transfer.

3.1 Six Tips to Keep Clients Coming Back for More

Getting new clients is an uphill task. But getting existing ones to hire you for another project is as easy as ensuring they are happy with your work.

Here are six things that will go a long way in splattering satisfied grins on the faces of your clients.

Write tailored proposals – Make it easy for a potential client to select you by tailoring each proposal to the project requirement. Customizing each proposal may be a time-consuming process for you, but it makes it a whole lot easier for the client. Making the extra effort is a win-win for you and the client.

Communicate effectively – Here are some basic communication DO's:

- Ask relevant questions before you take on the project. For example, who is the target demographic and who is the competitor? Asking questions at the beginning will help you understand the client's expectations and if you can fulfill them.
- Send regular updates to the client. If you are writing a report, submit the content in batches of few pages. If it's a series of articles, submit the articles in batches of two.
- Acknowledge all emails of the client within a couple of hours. As freelancers, it is natural to keep irregular hours. But checking your inbox regularly and sending a brief 'I will get back to you,' is all that is needed to buy time for a more detailed response.

Add value – There is an imminent danger in stopping at what you are hired to do. Eventually, the client will discover another freelancer who is willing to go a step further. If you want clients to hire again, you must go beyond the vanilla. Here are some suggestions for adding value to your clients –

- Submit your work as a well- formatted document
- Suggest multiple article headers which the company can use with various promotional material
- Include graphics/ images/ quotes/ statistics if it adds value to the content

- Add certificate of authenticity. For instance, place a Copyscape certified stamp on each document.
- Mention all sources of research at the bottom of the page
- Go beyond writing and offer constructive suggestions in other areas. What is your opinion of their website as a new user? Do you have suggestions for interesting Facebook posts for their business page?

Be courteous – Each client is different. For instance, some clients require frequent communication or may not be as forthcoming with sharing information on their business. A few may haggle on the project cost and others may take long to process invoices. Always be courteous and professional with your clients, regardless of the way a client interacts with you.

Ask for feedback – Positive feedback is the backbone of your freelance writing career. On the completion of each assignment ask clients for feedback. If you have done your job, most clients will be only too happy to post positive comments, which will appear on your profile.

But there will be that one percent which is unhappy. Ask for specifics of what wasn't as per expectations. Send an apology note to the client with proposed remedial measure for the next assignment. However, you can't please everybody. If you find that the client is unreasonable, move on.

Improve your skills – Add to your arsenal of competencies as a freelance writer. Here are some suggestions -

- List three books you will read this year to help you add to your skills
- Revamp your website
- Start a professional blog
- Learn new skills like designing an infographic, writing a grant proposal, or writing an e-newsletter.

3.2 Ten Email Tips When Working with International Clients

One of the most exciting aspects of being a freelance writer is the opportunity to work with clients of various nationalities. Most of customers on freelancing websites are from US, UK, Canada, and Australia.

There are discernible differences in the way people from different countries communicate via email. To ensure that you come across as professional and reliable in your email communications, follow these email etiquette guidelines when working with international clients.

Professional email opening and closing

- In India, it's the norm to begin business emails with 'Dear'. But some international clients (in the US for instance) may consider the use of the word too intimate. Opening an email with 'Hello', or just stating the person's name is considered an appropriate way to begin the email. Addressing a client with 'hey' is inappropriate for most business associations.

- Sign-offs have changed as well. 'Yours faithfully /sincerely' has been replaced with 'regards, 'Kind regards' or 'Best wishes.'

- As an email chain becomes more of an online conversation, it is okay to drop the salutations and the sign-offs, and just write the main message.

- Include key business information as part of the email sign-off (contact number, website, Skype and social media pages).

Informal maybe, but always meticulous

- The email subject should be the key message of the email. For instance, if you are sending a reminder to the client to clear a pending invoice, state that in the email subject.

- Avoid use of slangs as the acceptance of such words differs across cultures.

- Don't truncate words in an email like you would in an SMS text (For instance, using U for You). Avoid use of abbreviations even when sending an email from your smartphone.

- Ensure that there are no grammatical and spelling errors. If it is an important email, read it aloud to spot typos.
- Do not type in upper case (with the CAPS on), as it is interpreted as shouting.
- In business emails, use a smiley only if you know it will be received well. To be safe, let the client make the first move!

While the tone of your email communications may be friendly, remember that there is a business relationship at stake, and everything you do makes an impression.

CHAPTER 4: ADDITIONAL TIPS FOR WORKING AS A FREELANCE WRITER

4.1 Six Tips to Write Faster

For a freelance writer, time is money. One way to increase your earnings is to write more pages every day. Writing faster is also a way to make time for other facets of your life.

Writing fast will also help you write in your natural tone; it pre-empts the tendency to self- edit as you type.

Here are six proven methods for writing faster and being more productive every day.

1. Clear your thoughts

Before you start to write, spend a few minutes deciding what you are going to write. What is the topic of your article? What are the three key things your article will address? Don't start writing until you have listed your major ideas and collected your relevant research material.

2. Don't seek perfection as you write

Write the first draft of your article non-stop without stopping to correct your content. Write as clearly as you can, but leave the editing and the need to 'choose the right words' for a later stage. The best way is to write as if you are speaking to a friend.

3. Use online writing tools

Use the following tools to improve your writing ability, especially if you aren't very fast or accurate at typing -

- **Text expansion software**: Text expansion software works like the keypad on your smartphone. The software auto-completes words, phrases, and sentences basis your previously typed text. For example, you can create a trigger 'sig' which will auto-populate 'signature' as you type. Text expansion software works great if you are writing a large number of articles on a similar topic.

- **Voice to text software:** Some writers use voice to text software such as Dragon Naturally Speaking to dictate text to the computer, instead of using the keyboard.

- **Distraction-free text editor:** Write Box is a text editor that allows you to type as if you are writing on paper. There are no prompts to check spelling or correct the grammar so that you can write without any disruption.

The next three tips on writing faster may seem like the obvious ways to be productive, but we tend to ignore these all the time.

4. Determine your most productive hours

Most people are at their productive best in the morning. When you spend the first hours of you work day reading news websites and informative blogs, you lose the most productive time of your day. Shifting your 'browsing time' towards the end of the day may help you get more work done.

5. Set a timer for yourself

Pressurize yourself to write faster by allotting a time target to write a section of the article or the whole article. Running against the clock will discourage you from wasting time doing other things when you should be writing.

6. Eliminate distractions

Eliminate outside distractions while working. Don't check your phone and email for messages, and close the online chat window. If a friend calls in the midst of the typing spree, tell them you are busy and will call back. Obviously, this does not mean ignoring the important calls that need your immediate attention. But you need to focus on your work, while at work.

While the aim is to write more per hour, walk away from the computer every half hour or so to give your mind and body a break.

4.2 Start a Blog

As a freelance writer, you must have a blog. Blogging will make you a better writer, a better thinker, and a voice of authority in your field of interest. Blogging is an excellent way to share your knowledge with other writers and communicate with a wider audience.

What is a blog?

A blog is a website that contains various articles or 'posts' written in a conversational style. Once a post is published, followers and visitors to the blog can view the content, and give their feedback via online comments. The textual content of a blog is usually accompanied by images, videos and anchor text links (to other websites or blogs). A blog can be a personal blog started by an individual or a business blog that is part of the company's website.

You can start blogging for free on platforms such as WordPress and Blogger. You can customize your blog using the many free templates available on these platforms.

But to give your blog a touch of professionalism, create a domain name. Competition among the web hosting companies has ensured that domain registration costs are extremely affordable (under $20 a year). For instance, while rheagaur.wordpress.com is a generic name, ladybirdink.net is the registered domain name.

What should you blog about?

That's the fun part of starting a blog; you can blog about anything that is of interest to you. A blog can focus on a particular topic (e.g. a fitness blog), on multiple topics (e.g. a blog covering politics, environment and education), or on completely random topics (e.g. an individual posting on their life's events).

If it's a business blog, blog about your field of work. For personal blogs, choose topics that are of interest to you, or are inspired by your life's experiences.

How often do you need to blog?

Most bloggers struggle with an answer to this question. Some 'blog experts' advocate daily blogging; others advocate three to four posts every month.

The number of posts you want to publish a month depends on your goals for the blog. If the aim is to drive traffic, then you may need to blog daily or three to four times a week. But if your blog is your 'calling card' as a freelance writer to show your talent to future clients, then updating a new post once or twice a month will suffice.

You don't have to be a subject matter expert to start blogging. Keeping your blog content fresh and relevant will require that you research your central theme, which in turn will make you more knowledgeable.

It's important to be consistent both in content quality as well as content frequency (i.e. number of times you publish a post every week/ month). Here's why -

- Publishing your post on the same day of the week (rather than any day of the week) will improve your blog's SEO rankings.
- When you post on fixed days of the week and month, your readers know when you will be publishing next.
- Publishing high-quality posts is important to keep your readers hooked.

To ensure that you stick to the publishing schedule on your blog, write more posts when you have the time and schedule them for publishing at a future date.

4.3 Sixteen Online Apps for Your Freelance Writing Business

As a freelance writer, it's always a joy to discover apps that make work simpler.

Here is a list of sixteen online applications to ease your daily tasks.

Writing Apps

- **Copyscape:** Always pre-check your article on Copyscape for any plagiarized content. When you paste your article on Copyscape, it populates other articles that contain the same sentences. Go back to your article and rewrite the matching sentences so that it only has genuine content. For $5, you can buy 100 credits which will allow you to check 100 pieces of content. To save on credits, you can combine shorter articles and check about 1300 to 1500 words in one go (although the website recommends up to 2000 words per check).

- **Dictionary.com** – When unsure of word meanings, or if you are looking for synonyms/ antonyms, this is a helpful online dictionary.

- **Reverse dictionary:** Scratching your head for a word? Simply type the meaning and get a list of possible words.

- **Writebox_** – This is a distraction free text editor that allows you to write as if you were writing on paper. Using Writebox can improve your writing speed by as much as 20 percent. It also allows you to save files directly to Google Drive or Dropbox.

- **Hemingway App**: Use this app to make your writing concise and easy to read. The app identifies adverbs, passive sentences, difficult words, and complex sentences. It gives you an overall reading grade level for the content. For instance, a grade of 8, implies that anyone who studied up till 8th standard in school will understand your content.

- **Grammarly:** Use this app to identify grammatical errors as you type on email or MS Word. A crucial for every writer, the paid version costs about Rs.10000 for a year.

Content Development Apps

- **Google Adwords Keyword Planner**: Use this tool to identify keywords and keyword phrases for your article. Enter the necessary search criterion (country, industry, and proposed keywords) to identify words that have the maximum searches and lowest/ medium competition.

- **Keyword analysis** – Some assignments require a certain keyword density i.e. the number of times the keyword appears in the article. To check keyword density, just paste your content and article keywords on the website.

55

- **Bitly:** Use this tool to truncate lengthy links. Simply paste the extended link and the site populates a shortened link. For example:
  Before: https://adwords.google.com/ko/KeywordPl anner/Home?__u=7051450474&__c=1902981274
  After: http://bit.ly/14EPAG2

- **PDF converter** – Use any free software of your choice to convert word, excel and PowerPoint files into PDF. For instance, Nitro Cloud allows five free PDF conversions in a month.

- **Canva** – Canva allows you to design beautiful graphics and posters for blogs, social media, presentations, survey results and posters. You can edit the text in existing layouts.

Communication Apps

- **Dropbox :** This is an excellent way to share large files with a client and to create a back-up for your files. To upload, just drag and drop the file to the Dropbox account.

- **Skype:** Use Skype for calling and messaging international clients, as well as sharing files at low costs.

- **Ammyy:** This is a remote desktop sharing application that is easy to download and use. It's particularly useful for live demos. You can simultaneously communicate via Skype.

Business Apps

- **PayPal:** PayPal makes it easy to receive and track payments from international clients.
- **Vistaprint:** Use the website for designing business stationery such as cards, letterheads, business stickers, greeting cards, and marketing collaterals, at affordable prices.

4.4 Ten Business Promotion Tips for Freelance Writers

Freelance writing has its crazy moments, especially when you are juggling multiple assignments and have little time for anything else. But just when you seem to be enjoying the problem of plenty, your biggest client puts the project on hold. Suddenly it's the start of the month, and you have no work; the worst kind of feeling as a freelance writer.

Here's the important thing - Being an out-of-work writer doesn't mean that you should not be working. It's a reminder that you should never be complacent about your present work situation or of your writing skills.

Use the extra time to do things you normally struggle to find time for i.e. business promotion. Here is an infographic, aptly titled 'Business Promotion Checklist for the Out-of-Work-Writer'. It lists ten things you can do to promote your content writing services and improve as a writer.

Business Promotion Checklist for the Out-of-Work Writer

#1 Identify a new niche
Is there a new writing niche that you want to explore?
- Read websites in that category.
- Write a few articles in this new niche to include in your portfolio.

#2 Acquire new skills
How can you add value to existing clients or attract newer clients?
For example learn how to
- Design infographics, or
- Build a wordpress website.

#3 Update your portfolio
Contently is a great free platform to illustrate your writing.
- Create a writer's profile and upload articles (as links or PDF files) with images.
- Share your Contently profile link with clients.

#4 Update profile on freelancing sites
If you have been sourcing some work through freelancing websites, now would be a good time to revamp your profile - update skills, portfolio, services offered and profile pic

#5 Contact old clients

Contact clients you have worked for in the past
- Share your updated portfolio
- Highlight your new skills.

#6 Approach new clients

Contact potential clients in the new niche
- Pitch relevant topics with a brief outline of the article
- Include information on who you are and why you should be hired

#7 List on online directories

Update your business information on local and national directories.

#8 Schedule social media

Schedule posts for the next few weeks. Track insights to see which content attracts maximum reach. Also what is the best time for publishing?

#9 Revamp business logo

Do you have a business logo? Does the existing logo need to be revamped. Sites like Elance are a great way to find graphic designers at reasonable rates

#10 Update business card & website

Print business cards with the new logo and the new skills acquired. Ensure that your social media accounts and website carry consistent branding.

You don't have to do everything at once. All you need to do is schedule some time during your day to do at least one of these to ensure that you are rarely out of work.

CHAPTER 5: HOW MUCH WILL YOU EARN AS A FREELANCE WRITER?

You've bought this book and read about how to transition to freelance writing. Now you want a convincing answer to the fundamental question - **How much will you earn as a freelance writer?**

So let's get down to it.

As with any other self-owned enterprise, your freelance writing business will require time, effort, and perseverance. **The amount you earn as a freelance writer will depend on the following-**

- Your ability to write on different topics
- The time it takes you to write a single article
- The number of hours a week you can commit to writing for clients.
- Your ability to consistently deliver quality content and meeting committed timelines
- Keeping your customers happy

The more articles you write per week, the more you earn. The more your customers are happy, higher the chances of generating repeat and referral business. The higher your customer ratings on the freelancing websites, the more you can charge for your writing services.

The earning numbers below are from my experience as a freelance writer in India.

Stage 1: Monthly earnings within the first six months of freelancing

When you start, you may be paid $8 to $10 per 500 - 600 words, which is the typical length of a web article. In the beginning, it's difficult to win projects or to write more than one article a day. Even if you manage to earn just $100 to $200 from writing projects in the first couple of months, don't fret. Every job you do at this stage will help you win more clients in the future.

As you write more, the time it takes you to research information, collate thoughts and write a whole article, will reduce. Also, as you gain experience as a writer, by the fourth or fifth month you should start winning projects with greater frequency. If you work 22 days a month writing two articles a day, your earnings will be between $300 and $450 (or Rs.20000 to 30000) per month.

Stage 2: Earnings after one year of freelance writing

As you become a more experienced writer, you will find clients who are willing to pay a writing fee of $18 to $20 per page of 500-600 words. You can now earn $700- 800 (or Rs. 45000 to 52000) a month by writing 9-10 articles a week.

With time as you acquire expertise and graduate to more sophisticated article writing, your per article fee may increase to the $40-$50 range. You will earn $1000 (or Rs. 65000) if you write one article a day for 20 days in a month.

Even if your writing rate does not increase by as much as you would like, you will find that the time it takes you to write an article is substantially lower compared to when you first started writing. Now you can churn out more work for the same number of work hours, which will lead to increased earnings.

As you cultivate existing clients for more work, you must continue to bid for new projects. You can never have enough clients as a freelancer. Apart from writing content, you can now begin to diversify your business. You could write eBooks, acquire new skills such as website development, offer training for other aspiring freelancers, and work on improving your blog traffic.

When you work as a freelance writer, almost every day teaches you something new about your business. The better you get, the more you earn.

BE PREPARED FOR SPEED BUMPS ON THE WAY

One of the first things you will realize as a freelancer is that things don't go according to plan.

Don't keep waiting for the perfect moment to start! If you can't find the time to sit on your computer, make a small start. Spend a few hours a day to create your online profile, build a writing portfolio and start bidding for small projects.

Don't waste your time continuously checking your freelance account for reverts on bids placed, or for messages from clients. Use any spare time you have to do a lot more reading, improving your vocabulary, or updating your blog. Start reading blogs written by other freelance writers. Use your Facebook account to follow business pages of popular magazines like Entrepreneur, Inc Magazine, Mashable, The Wall Street Journal, and Fortune.

As a freelance writer, you will have periods of great luck followed by periods of lull, a fact that is often difficult to weather by those who have previously held a steady job. That's when you start hearing voices in your head – Did I make the right choice? Why isn't anyone responding? What am I doing wrong?

Remember that the obstacles in your way are just temporary speed bumps and not insurmountable mountains! Keeping faith in your abilities is half the battle won. Remind yourself of why you chose to become a freelancer – the desire to make a living from writing, to be your own boss, or the need to find a better work-life balance.

Being a freelance writer will help you develop skills such as pitching to a new client, negotiating pricing, creating a website from scratch, and using social media to drive business. And that's one of the biggest thrills – every day teaches you something in this line of work.

You will never know if freelancing is for you until you try it. Instead of quitting your job, do both. Work as an employee by day and moonlight as a freelancer by night for at least six months before you take the plunge. When you do become a full-time freelancer, ensure that you have adequate savings to cover monthly expenses for the next one year.

If you can stay self-motivated and are willing to put in the hard work to set up your business, the rewards will follow. All the best.

BOOK SUMMARY

CHAPTER 1: ARE YOU READY TO BE A FREELANCE CONTENT WRITER?

Freelance writing opportunities include the following:

- Website content
- Blogs
- Marketing Emails
- Social media updates
- eBooks
- Press release
- News summaries
- Brochures
- Promotional flyer
- Process manuals
- Training material
- Academic papers
- Reports
- Business proposals
- Product descriptions
- Company profiles
- Case studies
- Online quizzes

You need three core competencies to become a freelance business writer -

- An excellent command of written English.
- Ability to research topics on the web, and
- Ability to present information in a logical, easy-to-read manner

To be successful at writing for international clients, you need to develop additional skills:

- UK and US English
- Grammar and Punctuation
- Research
- Copywriting skills
- Professionalism
- Multi-tasking
- Positive attitude
- Familiarity with online tools
- Originality
- Time management

Life as a freelancer has its share of risks and rewards:

- The world is your competition
- You are the sole person in charge of everything
- It's a constant struggle to find business
- You earn only as long as you are working

- You get to work with international clients and write for different businesses
- Earn in dollars while working from home
- You choose whom you want to work with and how much work you want to take on.
- You can work from anywhere, anytime.

CHAPTER 2. STARTING AS A FREELANCE CONTENT WRITER

There are three important things you must understand when writing for the web:

1. Writing for the web is different from writing content for print.
2. Web content has to be search engine optimized –
   - Technique 1 – Focus on quality and frequency of content
   - Technique 2 – Include keywords, meta description, and anchor text
3. Style of writing varies with the type of web content. Buy the book - The Yahoo! Style Guide: The Ultimate Sourcebook for Writing, Editing, and Creating Content for the Digital World, to understand how to write for the web.

A few tips on writing your first batch of portfolio articles:

- Write topics you know
- Write from experience, but also do research.
- Include at least one anchor text link to another website of repute.
- Keep the writing style easy.
- Ask a friend or a family member to read your articles
- Upload your articles on sites like Contently and email the link to potential clients.

Using Freelancing Websites to Start as a Freelance Writer

Freelancing websites such as Upwork (formerly Odesk), Freelancer and Guru have made it easy for freelancers to reach clients all over the world. These are the types of content jobs available on Upwork under the category of writing.

- Academic Writing & Research
- Article & Blog Writing
- Copywriting
- Creative Writing
- Editing & Proofreading
- Grant Writing
- Resumes & Cover Letters

- Technical Writing
- Web Content
- Other – Writing

Five benefits of using freelancing websites

- Global reach with minimal cost
- Project management
- Secure payment
- Dispute resolution
- Opportunity to understand your competition

The cost of using freelancing websites has two components –

- Membership fee
- Website Commission

Eight tips on creating a stellar profile on freelancing websites:

1. Upload a professional picture
2. Develop a concise tagline
3. Describe your services, skills, and experience
4. Sell yourself, don't just describe what you do
5. Upload your portfolio
6. Take the skills test.
7. Ask for feedback
8. Reinvent your profile every few months

Ten tips for successful project bids-

1. Understand the project requirements
2. Know the client
3. Customize your proposal for each job
4. Attach relevant writing samples with each proposal
5. Propose a T + 1 timeframe for completion of the job
6. Be flexible in your pricing
7. Don't underbid for projects
8. Negotiate until you are comfortable
9. Don't take unpaid trial assignments
10. Don't stop bidding for better jobs

Five aspects to consider before working with a client

1. Project detailing
2. Client's communication style
3. Flexibility in approach
4. Price negotiation
5. Client's reputation

Should you have a writing niche?

A writing niche is important because it becomes your selling point, especially when you are pitching for work with new clients. But writing outside your niche makes you a better writer. Writing on broader topics also gives you a chance to widen your customer base. Choose a strategy that works best for you.

Five tips on how much to charge as a writer when your start freelancing -

1. Decide your most reasonable price
2. Review freelancing websites for how much others are charging
3. Charge higher if you have relevant experience
4. Consider the client relationship
5. Increase your fee gradually

Withdrawing your earnings

PayPal is a safe and quick way of withdrawing your money. Once the freelance website transfers the money to your PayPal account in US Dollars (USD), PayPal transfers the money to your bank account in the local currency, which takes less than five business days.

CHAPTER 3: KEEPING CUSTOMERS HAPPY

Six tips to keep customers happy:

- Write tailored proposals
- Communicate effectively
- Add value
- Be courteous
- Ask for feedback
- Improve your skills

Follow these email etiquette guidelines when working with international clients.

- Keep the email opening and closing formal
- The email subject should be the key message of the email
- Avoid use of slangs and abbreviations
- Ensure there are no grammatical and spelling errors
- Do not type in upper case

CHAPTER 4: ADDITIONAL TIPS FOR WORKING AS A FREELANCE WRITER

Six tips to write faster

1. Don't seek perfection as you write
2. Clear your thoughts
3. Use online writing tools
   - Text expansion software
   - Voice to text software:
   - Distraction-free text editor
4. Determine your most productive hours
5. Set a timer for yourself
6. Eliminate distractions

Start a blog

Blogging is an excellent way to improve as a writer, share your knowledge with other authors, and communicate with a wider audience.

If the goal is to drive traffic, then you may need to blog daily or three to four times a week. But if your blog is your 'calling card' as a freelance writer to show your talent to future clients, then updating a new post once or twice a month will suffice.

It's important to ensure content quality as well as content frequency (i.e. number of times you publish a post every week/ month).

Online applications for your freelance writing business -

Writing Apps
- Copyscape
- Dictionary.com
- Reverse dictionary
- Writebox
- Hemingway App
- Grammarly

Content Development Apps
- Google Adwords Keyword Planner
- Keyword analysis
- Bitly
- PDF converter
- Canva

Communication Apps
- Dropbox

- Skype
- Ammyy

Business Apps

- PayPal
- Vistaprint

Ten business promotion tips

1. Identify a new niche
2. Acquire new skills
3. Update your portfolio
4. Update profile on freelancing **websites**
5. Contact old clients
6. Approach new clients
7. List your business on online directories
8. Schedule social media posts
9. Revamp business logo
10. Update business card and website

Don't keep waiting for the perfect moment to start; make a beginning now!

End of the Book –

But a Beginning for You!

Note from the Author

Hello,

Thank you for buying my book.

If you would like to share your feedback on the book, or if you have any questions, please feel free to contact me through my website www.Ladybirdink.net.

I wish you the very best for your writing career.

Rhea Gaur